Skirting THE EDGE

I.B. ISKOV

Skirting the Edge

by

I.B. Iskov

Published by: In Our Words Inc./www.inourwords.ca

Editor: Cheryl Antao-Xavier

Book Design: Shirley Aguinaldo

Cover images: ©Billysiew ©Anker ©Bcritchley Dreamstime.com

Library and Archives Canada Cataloguing in Publication

Iskov, I. B., 1950-, author

Skirting the edge : poems / I.B. Iskov.

ISBN 978-1-926926-57-5 (paperback)

I. Title.

PS8567.S59S55 2015 C811'.54 C2015-906559-3

Some of the poems in this collection have appeared in The Canadian Jewish News; Voices of Israel 2008; Parchment, No. 15, 2008; Ascent Aspirations 2008 and 2010; Miracles & Meals Vol. 2; Holocaust Survivor Cookbook, Caras & Associates, 2012; ENCOMPASS II, Beret Days Press, 2013; Canadian Stories Magazine, Vol. 18, No. 104, 2015; and in some of the author's other collections including Sapphire Seasons [Aeolus House]; In A Wintered Nest [Serengeti Press]; After the Rain [Snowapple Press]; Space Alchemy [Passion Among the Cacti Press]; and Primitive Light, and She's All Around You, Beret Days Press.

'Rumour has it' won first Honourable Mention in Canadian Stories Magazine poetry contest, 2015 and in The Saving Bannister, 2015.

'Air Show' was published on-line – The Parliamentary Poet Laureate Poem of the Month, September, 2015 by the Parliament of Canada.

Dedication

For all my friends in poetry
who have given me their trust, friendship,
and golden words of wisdom.

Acknowledgement

Special thanks to Ronnie R. Brown for organizing my poems in the best order, setting them in sections, and for all her assistance and guidance in creating this book.

Table of Contents

Section 2 –Governmentality

Section 3 – Nocturnal Inspirations

SECTION I

Raw Beauty

The Moon Goddess

In her milk-white gossamer gown,
the moon goddess holds the golden glass.

Many suns rise in unison like bubbles
and vie for her attention;
but her eyes are fixed on the moon,
squarely set inside a mirrored circle
surrounded by silvery stars.

In the background
shimmering lights dance on water.

In one long stretch of an elusive flash,
the union of magic between heaven and earth
opens portals to the place of dreams.

The moon goddess never thinks of morning.
She caresses the winds of change
and understands her blanket of darkness
is suddenly removed in one sunlit moment.

She lifts her glass
reflecting the enigma of snow-pearls
pinned to her dress.

(Inspired by the painting "Moonlit Garden" by Peter Nixon)

Spirit Woman

From sun-shower dreams,
virgin stance ephemeral
in her cumulus gown,
the spirit woman waits hopeful.

Her ear to ear non-expression
dwells on the past.
Her mouth lies in darkness.
She has given away all her secrets.

Her hands, clenched in earnest,
escape attention. She laments
the smallness and all along
the spirit woman works them well.

With a virtue of detachment
she expects nothing.
Her feet, now ground-firm,
carry the weight of her shadow.

She conjures colours as a hobby,
shapes them into words and worlds.
Hair tousled by the wind,
the spirit woman remains free.

Martyred Mural

Ravens sit on a stone tower
surrounded by swelling shores.
Fishes flounder on silent shells.
There is no holy water.

Tired ghosts trudge wearily,
wait to be saved by a god
or a demon.

Sorrow bleeds on the canvas.
Marooned weeds cluster like lost children,
cling to barren mother earth.

Muted petrified wood lays still,
mimics unburied cadavers.

The sealed-in world of the dead
sits between clouds and oceans.

Statues of anonymous men
exhibit still life.
Vermillion flowers blossom like poppies
after the storm.

One can hear the dark bell of destiny
crossing over to the other side,
stars subdued, fragile as breath.

Pretentious Portrayals

The fullest expression of spirit must be judged as an article of customs rather than as a work of art. The equivalent of a souvenir bourgeois portrait is never humbled in a timeless house. When sunlight enters the room remarkably, a breath of intimacy bathes the face in its warmth, vaulting the portrait to new heights.

One feels helpless in a frozen state, admiring the work in the full atmosphere at a glance. The play of light allows the figure to come to life, whether birthed through the window or next to a burning candle or lamplight. When the figure is half-turned, a precarious notion of mystique is aroused. This pretentious portrayal strips the picture of intimacy, even though tarnished views bring notoriety and infamy to the artist.

After a hundred years have passed, the happiness the artist attempted to capture on the face turns stiff and stern, and even though it is aristocratic, joy is still displayed by the proud owner of the portrait. Thus, the collector, too, becomes pretentious, portraying an art critic without any scruples.

Silent Hillside

Single-leaf trees
sentry a non-existent world
of tall multi-coloured grasses.

No people inhabit this place
of lush mystery.

No stars litter
the cloudless magenta sky.

The artist,
brush in hand,
sits and paints one leaf
with amber persistence.

(Inspired by the painting by Itzchak Tarkay)

Asian Expressionism

Subtle heat in the lacquer of language
glazes over an inherited soft elegance.

A unique cosmetic mystique makes-up pictures
of guileless innocence,
the promise of a sidelong glance.

The seductive glow of peach-bloom flesh
lures our attraction to elusive loveliness.

Lush profusion of emerald and gold performs
an exquisite marriage of ethereal pleasure.

Loving dialogue is repeated in folk crafts,
pottery, poetry, porcelain and paintings.

A few simple lines create a mood of longing.

They gather restless whispers, set them aflame,
finally allowing the embers to drift across the pages.

A few simple strokes of a brush depict
samurai, goblins, beauties, foreigners and demons
in an austere dreamland of wonder.

Spring blossoms in a floating world,
ephemeral beauty, the desired truth.

Aztec Paradise

Acolytes attend to the water goddess
in syncopation with the tide.

Tlaloc, the rain god, is rich in colour
and is the most splendid of all.
Surrounded by fluttering butterflies,
he oversees the water cult.

The water goddess sprouts plants
from her head, knowing they will germinate
and soon create a magnificent garden
in the kingdom of hallucinogenic beauty.

Tiny fire-frescoed figurines frolic in streams,
play ball, carry one another piggyback
and splash in the water.

This scene of watery abundance is a paradise
for those who died by drowning.

Celestial Studio

I imagine what God's art studio must be like.

Large and white, between boundless clouds,
His studio contains palettes of silver and gold
to prime canvasses of light and shadow.

In another corner, His kiln stores the raw materials:
amber dust, rain, and baby's breath.

Each life form lovingly held
in His hands; at our creation,
painstakingly molded each of us
with delicate precision.

We are flawed but beautiful in His eyes.
No sculptor has yet produced a perfect statue.

Even those primal experiments
resulting in imperfect people are viewed
as sacred and dear in His eyes.

Raw Beauty

Poignantly pointed at surreal discoveries,
my virtual camera paints personal passion

solitary, kooky, with prophetic undertones,
framing famous secrets of domestic life.

Compositions of everyday people are quickly frozen
in time-capsule photographs.

Like a sleuth I discover the extraordinary
on downtown streets and in a city park.

The face of society removes its mask
and bares its soul in Technicolor.

Narrow confines of civilization are broadened discreetly
and displayed in an exaggerated pictorial canon.

Never missing a moment,
the camera's eye and mine share history.

His World of Art

"Work is love made visible." — Pablo Picasso

Life was bitter and good like the Italian journey
when a poor opera inspired a poor artist.
A sympathetic response sparked within him.

He was catapulted periodically throughout each decade
as he stood before his easel pouring heart into his paint.

Devoted to Olympian isolation,
he let the angels crowd his landscape.
This is when his most varied works came forth.
They were grouped together
and stacked in separate strong-rooms.

His hidden treasure, gloom-smitten,
mirrored his own reflection.
He would observe his subjects from a distance
under the spell of Bohemian voices.

The unknown Spaniard's revolutionary style
is depicted in hundreds of pictures.
He blended adventure with whimsy,
inspiration with ingenuity,
creativity with unconventionality.

In his world, everything had its place and pattern.
His house and his garden were his models,
watched, thought about and finally,
turned into other forms in his mind
and brought to life on canvas.

Always gregarious, yet always seeking seclusion,
he would sketch his pet pigeons
from the third floor balcony of his flat
on the Mediterranean.

His natural gaiety filled the air,
except when his longing for Spain made him homesick.
This is when he would work without a break of any kind,
disappear into a studio corner
and create paintings, or woodcuts, or engravings,
or sculptures, or etchings, or ceramics
long past midnight,
straight into the dawning hours of morning.

When asked which "period" of his career
was his favourite –
Blue, or Rose, or Cubist, or Nihilist, or Realist –
Pablo's reply was, "The next one."

The Wicked Prince of Painters

Rembrandt van Rin lived in a golden cage.
Fantasy-rich, he stole his first wife's dowry,
cheated on his taxes and seldom paid his bills.

Ignominy quickly vanished with the stroke of a brush.
He wielded power like a blue-blood,
swift and sure of himself and his art.

Fun-loving, charismatic and completely disreputable,
his genius shone like a precious stone under candlelight.
He used luscious colours
to illustrate both agony and ecstasy.

With loving care and precision,
this master created clear, stunning images
of all mankind.
Gorgeous crimes were committed
both on and off the canvas.

He owned a sense of bravado, briskly confident
thinking about his next financial scam.
Storm clouds could not quell his spark of defiance.

At the pinnacle of his career, this prodigal son
reigned free of a conscience in the midst of high praise.
Twisted schemes and vile actions enhanced his art.

Rembrandt's sins demanded a higher price
than his work.
One self-portrait depicts a wreck of a man,
a deposed ruler.
The disgraced prince of painters died
a pauper.

Uncultivated Sculptures

Renaissance gold
shines a legend.
The chaste territory,
a whitewash of colour.

The ground outside
houses small temples,
columns impregnate clouds.

One behind the other,
in interior woods
more practical than beautiful,
eccentric iron fences spread
across immeasurable dimensions.

The density of inhabited distance
is a perpetual drone
with no current possible.

I taste the wind burst local,
gust Neanderthal laughter,
caressing stones and earth.
There are no sad trees.

The Art of Film Noir

Deliberately blurring boundaries
appeals to contemporary beliefs.

First-hand accounts remain good quirky examples.
They promote ambiguous clarity.

Forbidden fruits are produced
in a still life movie industry.

As in a painting, they are viewed as visual motifs.
Brief scenes are drawn modest and dazzling.

High-angle views illustrate free-ranging techniques
designed by the director's keen eye.

Avoiding traditional form and style,
the treatment of progress remains prominent.

Ambivalent attitudes jump out in fits
and starts.   There is desire.

Sometimes confusing, these films need an expert
to explain the rough-edged workmanship.

Figures of betrayal are shown in silhouette.
They don't seek to change the audience's ways of thinking.

Like the painter's brush, the camera moves in,
brings stylized portrayals back to life

and then fades;
but only until meaning and impact are portrayed

poignantly in the climax.
Preconceived notions are forsaken by all viewers.

Interweaved Art

Rare and extraordinarily beautiful,
created by many Persian hands,
my tapestry of many colours
laboured into the world,

traveled across an ocean
companioned by other rare
and extraordinarily beautiful rugs.

Never hung on a wall,
my prized acquisition,
framed by silken fringes,
illuminates with the sun
sedately and refined
on my living room floor.

My Universe

Green and white velvet sculptures
fade discretely in the morning sun.

The silver dust sprinkles soft
on mahogany
while swollen fingers
embrace the slender needle
and play a silent song of silk.

The embroidery sings
in tranquil tones of earth and sky.

I sit barefoot in the picture,
dig my splendid toes
in the gentle browns
like a gardener
in a tropical oasis.

I patiently create
my universe,
the eternal stitches
a small immortal gesture
never to be forgotten
like a tender lullaby
or a kiss.

Carving the Dance

The body blooms and shines
like the luminosity of a warrior's faith.
It lifts and moves with the breeze,
gracefully careening over graves
of ancestral bones.

Spiritual pleasure is derived
inside cylindrical bark containers.
Highly stylized faces adorn long wooden stems
like flower-faces reduced to ears, brows and nose.

One must listen for the laughter
hidden inside the dancer.
He leads you out of the sunlight
into dark places of inner blackness
and lets you see the Fang of Gabon.

Spiritual growth is transformative energy
empowering the sculptor while educating the soul.

(Inspired by a wood carving of a ceremonial paddle from Easter Island)

Heraldic Art

Unique broad and thin shapes
fill given space in a formline.

Powerful, uninitiated speculations with tapered ends
attain an evolutionary closure.

Whatever the ovoid story, there is always a tension
controlling and manipulating agile fingers.

In dense habitats, creatures are squeezed
until they become rigid
forcing them to shed their own skin in a timeless matrix
of gold   or of silver   or of wood   or of slate.

Spirits inhabit a magical palace.
Every child's dream of fantasy holds a rendezvous.

In this realm, birds have four feet,
frogs have prominent mouths,
wide rows of teeth
and long, leathery extended tongues.

In the centre of this enchanting vast, cosmic system,
supernatural animals separate earth, sea and sky.

The all-important emerge and are revered.
Ceremonial life and mythology
interconnect in a dramatic aura.

Little watchful humanoid faces climb out.
They speak of a lingering primordial relationship,
deliver a miracle where intricacy and intimacy marry
and live happily forever after.

(Inspired by the carvings of Bill Reid)

The Culture of Native Art

Hidden amongst skyscrapers
and monster high-rise glass buildings,
in shadowy recesses sprinkled throughout North America,
an ancestral connection initiated by Haida carvers
still prevails.

Beginning with the birth of the raven,
expressions of beauty were carved with romantic energy,
tinged with darkness out of loneliness and alienation.

Extraordinary acts of faith
displayed on old poles in native villages
are punctuated by songs of Manitou.
Massive totem parks and museums
in no smooth patterns,
conserve and protect the mythical
in a vanished heritage.

The eagle and the bear reside comfortably
in a large clamshell.
Boxwood maple totem poles
conceal their homes intricately.

Order and control cannot prevent the raven
from stealing the limelight.
Stretched to the limit,
a broken beak turns out quirky surprises.
Gravity-bound,
matter and spirit rise
to challenge time and change.

There is an aura of sentiment
and an aching nostalgia connected to the art,
making it monumental.

The Sphinx of Giza

The part human, part animal idol stretches
across sand-swept desert with refinement.

Carved out of living rock,
the Sphinx never sleeps.
He is ever-watchful over the pyramids,
knowing one day,
the pharaohs will return
and rule the world once again.

Eyes averted to the skies,
the Sphinx knows there will be a sign
from the sun-god Râ.

Perhaps a mighty rainbow will appear,
or maybe, a lightning bolt will shatter
the mortuary monuments

and all of Egypt's great leaders will emerge,
one by one,
and restore the Sphinx
so he may rise from his post,
seek much-craved shelter
and have a long-awaited nap.

The Art Building

I dream of a new wonder for the world
the public would not measure,
architects would take centuries to construct.

I imagine lavish rooms
with ornate molding, elegant chandeliers,
hand-woven rugs on shiny marble floors,
one-of-a-kind masterpieces
exhibited side-by-side on all the walls.

With binoculars pressed against my face,
I compass my vision
inside the framework.

Like a seasoned photographer,
I encapsulate fantastic footage of
the most colossal art building

strategically built on safe soil,
far from madness and mayhem,
between two towers near coastal waters
close to commerce and world trade.

Far from completion,
rough terrain resembles burnt clay
in a disturbing myriad of urban debris
and post-mortem landmarks.

You Know It When You See It

Steel zigzags,
stained glass sunburst,
aerodynamic linear chevrons
on lacquered wood
comprise a tiny part of Art Deco.

With a sleek aesthetic,
symmetrical geometric shapes
in yellow, purple, ruby and turquoise
adorn everything from architecture to jewelry.

Angular patterns embellished
with diamonds and onyx
on exotic, eclectic works of art
are worn on walls and bodies.

From flapper girls to poster girls,
vivacious moods are captured
and turned into vogue.

With a fascination all its own,
a spirit of frivolity echoes
Deco Deco Deco
all over the world.

The Sex of Art

To understand any sexual figurine, one needs to undress quickly, stand on a wooden platform and think only of the Renaissance. By making use of nude bodies in picturesque portrayals, political opinions stray from the scene and become the pinnacle of pre-mature porn. However, large breasts and buttocks need no hype. Anyone with a vivid imagination will deliberate, then finally masturbate inside the hallowed canvas. Biblical, mythological and psychological traumas resulted from missing arms and heads; those models worked shorter shifts. The most prolific sexual heroes display anatomically correct genitalia: the classic peep show in realism. Polaroid polarities are developed when various vicarious virgins separate the painter from the saint and imagine voyeurism as neo-classicism in ten seconds. The very frisky fresco is restored by loving hands; flesh and blood are recreated by arrangement. When sex is placed high above an ancient palette, you know it is time to visit your local art gallery and witness moments of ecstasy on purely naked walls.

SECTION 2

Governmentality

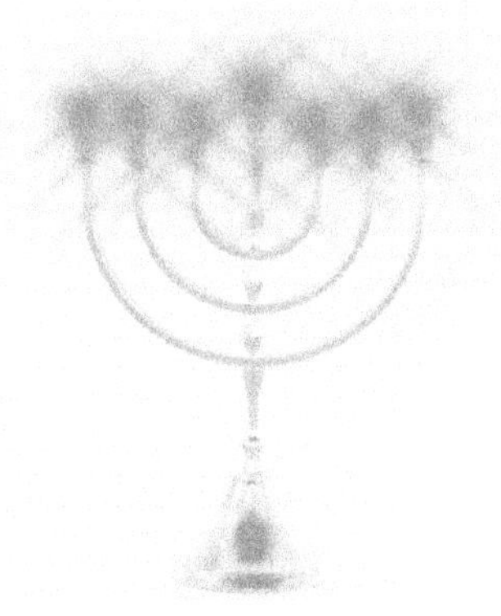

Before The Flood

Once, when the earth was young
and Eden just a garden,
the names of clouds were only a sigh.

Once, when the smallest shiver
wafted through autumn,
a fashion statement resonated in basic green.

Once, when no shame and life
were contained in a breath,
each moment ignited in a glimpse
between mouths full of fruit.

Once, while everything still
was fresh and naïve,
the twilight brimmed a rainbow
of benevolence and gold.

Once, when my man was just a boy
and terror a horror movie,
each peace protest from a flower child
sang a new era.

Once, when buildings were giants among men
and the telephone a dynamic lifeline,
gentle shadows hushed a tableaux of fury
between flightless flora and fauna.

Once, when beasts were confined to zoo cages
and communism the perfect enemy,
rain-soaked and dramatic
iron fear curtained a new born question.

Once, when snakes could walk the earth
and apples promised wisdom in a bite,
the air harnessed a rhapsody of fire.

Governmentality

Every important rock spent
headfirst like unbearable heat
burns holes through tweed,
propels the establishment
to be taken for granted.

The political future of growing up
in a cycle of deliberation
eventually shuts down
daycare centers and hospitals.

Many escape in complete control
by resisting mental ghosts
while they extend loans
to escape foolproof reckoning.

Ordinary rituals are wearing thin.
Dreams dangle on loose tongues
while over the past several decades,
the perfect pioneer
is undermined and deregulated.

North America's New War

The hostile breath of war
inhales and exhales
in black and white under metal gray.

Frontiersmen knowingly wait
for gunfire, bombs, the lethal germ,
singing freedom songs
gallantly forged from dust.

No uniforms expose the enemy.
No heavy boots parade shaky, neutral grounds.

Angry faces shout anti-American slurs,
worship posters of Hitler in a beard,
sport suicide vests under accoutrements of hate,
call themselves oppressed heroes.

Cube vans with tinted windows
race on deconstructed roads at 2 a.m.,
transport harbingers of death
to hidden laboratories.

The militia murder joggers, airline passengers,
children in school-yards and universities,
coffee house patrons, subway and bus travelers,
and afterwards,
throw parties, celebrate their victories
and pay homage to a sinister god.

What is a Jew

I wear a veneer of skin.
This does not transpire at birth
but rather in the dark chapter of time
when the sun glowers without heat
and despair descends like hail
covering hope, leaving an impasse.

I no longer expect tolerance
when I prepare latkes,
light my Shabbat candles
and pray for peace and goodwill.

My clothes are curtains
concealing subtle innuendos
locked inside rooms of memory.
Sometimes, my fingers part the flimsy fabric
and another offensive event occurs.

There are synonyms used
to describe a Jew.
I collect and fold them inside newsprint
and bury them in a deep hole
in my heart.

Praying

A narrow wish
on the tip of my tongue
divides
each time my heart rocks.

Hope surrounds me, like a stole
under the hammock heavens –
sadness hardens to stone.

I want the clouds
to remember the past,
heal scars
in the sweep of space.

I want to believe
in institutions,
feel safe
amidst broken stars.

I want to believe
in light and crowns,
in filaments of Mitzvahs.

I pray,
remaining close to my faith;
muse ancient passages
mirrored in English.

Holocaust Cemetery

Grass and mud mingle
in trodden sorrow
around the granite.

Beloved names
of the dead
etched in Yiddish,
like a story by Sholem Aleichem
written in Auschwitz.

Engraved columns
bitterly sleep
on a slate grey landscape
in the orphaned park
without a voice
or a dream.

The sun is buried too
under swollen clouds
the compressing sky
near tears
and the wind clings
to my legs
like a frightened child.

The air is in pain
its dull white grasping breath
makes the minutes crawl
in naked trembling silence.

(On visiting the Zaglembier Monument)

Where is She?

Half-smiling, a young woman stands in sepia tones,
her light brown hair coiffed like Garbo's.

My mother, in her better memory, confessed:
This is my sister, Basha. She was my father's favourite.
Isn't she beautiful?

My sixteen-year-old brain racing,
I wondered why
my mother never told me
about this other auntie,
about her husband,
my other uncle
and their two daughters,
my other cousins.

I wondered why
I never got to visit them
and why my mother's parents never mentioned
this important person,
their eldest and most attractive, intelligent daughter,
all the years they lived in Canada
after the war.

I looked at my mother, full of questions
and asked only one:
Where is she?

My mother, wiping tears, blurted:
She was murdered by the Nazis
with her husband and children.

Displaced

The small yellowed star reads
"details hardly matter."

I write the history on tender knees –
tired skin imprinted on damp earth
holding concrete crumbs in fundamental darkness.
The weight of one palm balances contradictions.

Blank walls behind my closed eyes are so wide.
I feel small tricks slope away
altering cinematic views.
I know there are possibilities.

I hold my breath
sick of familiar signs, human arrogance,
emotionless   laugh
on the outside
search the wanton earth for details.

Like a butterfly on a tulip   I   jump the gap
suspended   between
the suit and the case.

Perhaps it is only the cavity of my existence.
Perhaps I'm going crazy.
Where are you going?
You know there's a war.

Old skin in my worn coat
turns a corner.

Candle Lighting

I am self-taught in the art
of memorized magic
ancient incantations
ignite in a moment,
bloom at once.
Bright yellow flickering petals
spike halos,
run off into the air.

My grandmother would be proud
again and again,
lighting her candlesticks,
praying respectfully
with mellowed hands
weighted with worries
beneath salt water and scars.

My Hebrew is a pretense
I have created myself
wrapped in a Canadian shawl
on a dead end street,
moving lips in moral denial.

A thick fabric of warmth
shades precious
still.

Be On Guard

Someone scrawled
a large SWASTIKA
while the world blew up
and the tired eyes of saints
filigreed – gagged scared.

The moon swings like a hammock
repeats strangled rage
burning tomorrow's pain
step-by-step.

Don't lower your eyes,
don't cross
anyone in an over-sized sweatshirt
toppling Jewish tombstones
muttering Mein Kampf in prayer,
don't cross
to the other side.
Fierce heat
bright like morning sun
blinds internally
cruel and hard.

Move slowly
pebble by pebble.
Count the feet of your oppressors.
Invisible barriers of indifference
constructed in the mind
whisper protests when there is
standing room only for dissidents.

Hire a bodyguard
big and black and muscular
with arms bearing a tattooed Cross
as big as a SWASTIKA.
Strategically place him at the front door
of your temple.

Boat People

Hunger crowds the illegal passage.
Precarious company awaits liberty
all over the world.

Morning appears like death,
gaunt and grey
on the apertures of angst.

The sun hides behind clouds,
shares heat with the moon
in seclusion.

Immigrants intertwine foreign
language and cigarettes
smoking and fuming.

Ragged children the only distraction.

Cold and needy,
tired sheep are led to the ark
seeking a distant salvation.

Boat people execute their freedom
slowly sinking under the horizon.

Doomsday Sage

Terror is the invasion of peace.
Human hurricanes of doom
shard shell-shocked streets.
There is no unbiased room.

In a bomb blast, I fade into white,
live days one by one.
I pretend there is a heaven
when my life is done.

In periods of silence,
I sense my impending demise,
swallow the whole magilla.
Dark glasses shield my star-struck eyes.

In skimpy hours, the earth is sullied.
Air spills loose like broken beads.
Nothing can hide the ominous truth.
No one cares about my needs.

And when the wind whistles low
on long, deserted streets,
someone utters another idiom
the media repeats.

On Patrol

I walk away every time
like an invisible bride,
leave no white footprints.

This is no accident.

I walk away every time,
the fragile amnesia
continues
lighting inside.

I walk away every time.
I haven't changed.
Always another sound
knocking my eyes in panic.

I walk away every time
there is a terrible war.
Strange sentences secret structures,
the carnivorous cling,
fevered in shadows.

I walk away every time
behind the door
my liberty is isolated
from pedestrian life
and death.

Though My Voice Breaks

I tread invisibly
like a specter,
shaking graves
in heavy shadow.

Listening to fog
in the distance
I am earthbound.

Stars are combing the trees.
I hide beneath my sheltered vision,
newborn wren
in a wintered nest.

Boldly utter stillborn sayings:
know the world will never
change. There is no rebirth,
no emergence.

I am a wingless creature
on a hard impenetrable ledge.

Based on Research

Behind exotic veils,
trembling truths emerge.
Violently understandable,
arbitrary strict rules leave nothing out.

Certain flaws in foreign customs
run, trip, tackle, smash and slap.
In a circle of bloodied shame,
unrepaired damage is neglected.
Forever scarred, silence is repeatedly raped
between fabrics of anguish and oppression.

Religious hostility is hidden
inside a dismembered clump of bone
throbbing behind thick walls
where machetes thwack in the dark.

In liquored denial, fundamental rights
are knocked down, punched, kicked,
bludgeoned, strangled, burned
beyond recognition.

Sacred Legends

Broken hearts bleed gentle
heat up the clarity
seed efficiency
fierce courage
through loneliness
the antiquated silence
leaks beads of time.

Small bones
under shedding skin
wait for a new voice
in the dark
conceal brittle memories
protected by shadows
swollen with arthritic patience
heaving loud.

In the quiet
childhood nightmares
fade in flight
erode in fields of flowers
unearth the soil
unmask hollow souls
draw cold hate
the shivering smiles
eye barren gardens
beneath a naked sky.

From the turmoil
of tongues
rough-blanketed
purging red
the legends distil
leaving an evaporated legacy.

Sacred Wood

I need a pious charm
carved from orchards,
hand rubbed,
bright like burning glass.

It is just the thing to take
when the weather is overhead,
        the garden barren,
        the road intense,
        the dream unremembered,
        the heart swollen,
        the night stomached again.

The polished ebony
would candle a flame
like a fount curling over rock.

The moonlight's ritual sparkle is a specter in solace.

I split wood on cool days.
I work alone by the book.
In the pitch of darkness,
the naked stillness is memorized on scrolls
in a prominent place for supplication.

The timbered talisman,
my apologetic panacea
nailed to my forehead.
This certain hallmark
my consolation for fancy.

Glass House

Sunlight falls on dusty shelves.
One silver goblet begs for shine.

Candlesticks, erect as sentries,
guard the precious paradise.

I open my cabinet doors,
rearrange familiar figurines,

hide what's missing,
chipped or broke.

I care for moments,
dust them off, display them
on little easels.

I'm composed.

Memorial

The world crawls somewhere
under a sinking sky
large and hollow
beyond touch.

The whole long truth
falls tenderly
in sorrow.

Shtetl after shtetl
impaired logic
steals
a chunk of hungry earth.

The world spins
cradled-in-a-cry
bloated and
perspiring.

The forlorn assemble
in meeting halls
with hope and devotion
sharing history.

Skirting the Edge

Transparent plastic bags
smother my dreams
like second-hand smoke.

I am very small,
unable to translate the silence.
Static air combusts
rude and bullish.

Someone long-winded
follows me around,
holds me responsible.

This is when sorrow
is etched on a stone heart
no one ever sees.

No One Believes More

This was part of the dispute:
many men were out fighting
loaded with crowns
and old arguments.

Flaccid flames fanned ready tongues
with delicate precision.

And in the same breath,
shrugged and spit and coughed
out of the barrow
groped with twig-like fingers
in a mess of light,
strangled wisdom.

Tight fistfuls of language
clenched unheard advice
in cold, bitter skin,
denied everything.

Big Game

I went hunting for a heart.
Wrote about problems
always the reflection
of a stark-naked hurting
for the long things in life.

I went hunting for a moral
in a crowd of smothered stars
knowing it takes time
to surrender misgivings.

I went hunting for a reason.
Discovered sentences lying in green pastures
late at night blanketed by darkness.

I went hunting for a promise.
Climbed stairwells and ladders.
Searched for language not yet spoken
on a brilliant slivered afternoon,
witnessed the death of conversation.

I went hunting for an answer,
crouched over my problems
like a private detective magnifying issues.
This made the meaning of obscurity even smaller.

I went hunting for acceptance.
I am not alone.

Freedom Space

The sun sails over the continents
outfoxing the imperial
intelligentsia.

Worn fleets pretend importance.

What a spectacle.
A gust transports
one red balloon
on its back, flees
with a child's infectious laughter
while below, people wheedle while
the national security surrounds history aiming guns.

I'm not protesting.
To vanguard the heads of states
encoded in blue and yellow
and not care if any of them
refuse to look up
(though it would be novel)
this is when I'd grant
a full pardon
and freedom space for all.

All Smiles Are Rainbows

We have had two thousand years
to stumble and lean
squawk great cries
detached and horrible
clamor for attention
carry on like a hyena
then retreat to the corner
with a quiet that could be taken for patience.

We have had two thousand years
in the cold
behind the fence
fixed under the cover of cloud
in troubled silence
to worry about the clinging terrors
of everyday life
in a landscape that could be taken for paradise.

We have had two thousand years
to point broken fingers
in the summer heaviness
spin anger
spew up air furious
meet triumph in the gutter
wait for sun and light
from a window that could be taken for vision.

We have had two thousand years
to sing like thunder
dissolve chaos
touch into wholeness
bind hearts together
fill the air with promise
spirit   commitment   resilience
in peace that could be taken for a miracle.

Under The Leaden Sky

The cold crudely clumps inside wind
on brutal nights,
ices labyrinths in the dark.

Six-pointed stars arrested,
sealed in principled prisons,
await liberation
by stoic underground movements.

Fragile, precious
antique silver mezuzahs
behind barbed wire fences;
careful reactions pattern shame.

The authority of order
mighty as a skyscraper,
stubborn as a hurricane,
stalwart as a terrorist.

I fight City Hall,
demand mountains be climbed,
insist concrete airplanes
be awarded less gravity.

I want to wade through the windy warren
while naked parchment whimpers
timeless through dark dreams
in a secret spring.

Rumour Has It

I am addicted to decaf coffee
and newspaper rooms where
I pour over the print
for proper digestion of the news,
though in these terrorist days
every good story proves volatile.

Rumour has it I work
on the median behind the traffic sign
buried under history books
with compatible companions
sticking to their cell phones.

We discover the repetition
at our feet – Hitler and the ISIS
with equal disgust.

Moving from the grey matter
of fact to a bomb shelter
on the lakefront covered with black cloth
would keep me from staying home;
but this is no dry run.
I return at moonrise
and wash up on a sheltered beach.

My collaborators believe I hold the pencil
like a knife,
but they only whisper the reality:
"Any woman climbing on her knees
is never at a loss for words
and should be held responsible
for the gossip."

It is my custom to venture out
in the wilderness,
set myself on a mad course to organize
nouns and verbs and eggshells;
maybe even broken glass.

But I don't fantasize a happy solution.
Jews and dogs and good Christian children
are all susceptible to the same fate.
Brute creation demands this.
Ask any executioner holding a gun.

SECTION 3

Nocturnal Inspirations

Poetry and Politics

Imagine politicians debate
wearing turtleneck sweaters and berets
in coffeehouses.

Perhaps a performance is coming.

The crowd holding pencils behind cardboard boxes
waits in sun-glassed boredom for the word.

Restriction plays tight
censorship in metaphor
even Yeats and Trudeau
still go on and on.

Their thoughts suffer no death.

The energy penned in the Promised Land
a dimension deep
emotional repetition every four years.

Some of the best poetry
was composed right before election day.
Idyllic idealism sputtered
in front of the microphone
like a quenched roman candle.

It was great while it lasted.

Papers erode and the word vanishes
in my memory
the stars live their work
in duplicate and triplicate.

Every time another politician stands
he clutches shovels and boulders
and another poem constructs the truth.

Looping for Art's Sake

I delve into that place
illustrated in my mind,
groping for that link

to loop everything together
long-short   fast-slow
tender-struck
nebulous and cultural.

Imagining myself an artist,
I envision a great eclipse.
Black is the predominant mood.

With tired fingers,
I spiral my pen for a strong therapeutic effect.

Looping can be very beautiful
in just the right light.

Letters become complex acrobats,
empower the paper-stage with
confrontational comic calamity
never fracturing their naiveté
lest they transform themselves
into something truly grotesque.

Stylish looping is an acquired skill.
An inordinate amount of time is spent
repeating the basic fundamentals
to fulfill true penmanship.

I manage to pronounce each O with enthusiasm
without compromising the metaphor.

I want to be in the loop.

To Take an Oak Tree for a Mentor

requires deliberation
vigorous leaning on this shoulder takes caution.

I'll whittle time with him tonight.

Below the crown, my left side tips
against his silent bark;
we become
leaf and stem messengers –
muted green thinkers.

Golden fleece spills
from twisted branches
for pollination, lichen habits
climb light-headed,
glimpse the persuading ground.

My thoughts cling to the roots
deeply embedded in
the heart of the matter;
wait for sun and inspiration,
sprout naked fragments.

All Those Old Songs

I live backstage
behind the scenes
behind the limelight
without the kaleidoscope.

But it isn't real theatre.
I never had a performance.

My heart beats rhythm
like a metronome.

No fully automatic system
performs all those old songs
sealed in square plastic cases.

All my scratched records lie
inside torn jackets.

They just don't fit in anymore.

Backstage Debris

I would like to be the projector
clicking carefree construction in concert
cast true neon noise.

I would like to be the radio playing
nostalgic old music
swirling sweet in the distance
like the moon beyond grasp
in a star-flash memory.

Time and timely intellectual things are short-lived.

The sun glimmers elusive gold
in a blinding and perfect paradise.

Wet things stir inside sterile throats
until the ever-after sigh puffs tiny
haloes in silent spaces.

A cosmic catharsis cankers the psyche
and ubiquitous grievances fester
like deep-rooted wounds in cornered limbs.

Melancholia is trapped inside old bones
buried by dogs in misbegotten forests;
new ideas, like weeds, grow unnoticed.

I stuff one pocket with crumpled paper
subconsciously clenching catharsis
and naming it writer's block.

Air Show

Mid-afternoon
mid-January
mid-sky

a host of Starlings frolic
on a dull grey cloud-scape

The bird-ensemble
unfurl wings
like black orchids blooming

joyfully coast
back-and-forth
dance-on-air
in formation
fashion
rings and hearts

over the intersection
at Finch-and-Yonge
entertaining a crowd
of cars

Retro Revisionism

Booming rock music
heavy on weed
blossoms in a psychedelic summerhouse,
luxuriating in raucous revelry.

Bikers with mindless tattoos
congregate outside a bar,
their chain mail clanking
like empty beer cans.

Residual replays on the radio
swarm the hours
like flagrant vagrants fading
at the end of each song.

Ballet Lessons

Before I went to kindergarten
before I could roller skate
before I could read the time
before I could sing the alphabet
before I had anything else but baby teeth
I could dance ballet

Perfectly

I would raise my arms above my head in an arc
I would gracefully stand on my tiptoes
and pirouette
and pirouette
and pirouette
and pirouette
across Kildonan and Main
when the light was red
and my mother would scream my name
and run after me
and get hit by the car
and almost die.

Autumn's Grandeur

When the sun breaks open the blue,
a flame dances through clouds
in frosty dawning
birds blossom outside my window
little by little the day slowly thaws.

Trees let loose their coloured garments,
empty pockets of rain.
Emerald puddles sparkle
through the wind's reflection
in the cool of morning.

Rain-smell arrives with the wind
warm water-beads cascade,
adorn October's fading green blanket.
In the wide yellow light
squirrels scamper loose
and blow across the fence.

All summer was heat in steaming reflections
warm beads of sweat imitated the rain,
pretended to nourish grass and birds
found shade in tired branches.

I cannot measure the size of sky,
blue beyond the light.
Above pale clouds, soaring geese
in a line, one by one
move under the weight of the sun
through Heaven's water barrels.

When the whole day is washed clean
and trees paint their gowns yellow,
the autumn sunset will radiate history
among barren fields and skyscrapers,
then lazily burrow under the stars.

The Jewish Side of the Poem

The composition is gathered
like freshly cut flowers.

A too-pretty bouquet
admired a short time
bewitching   before wilting.

I press dried phrases of pink and beige
between the stanzas
to make the poem flat.
Punctuation must be clean and germane.

Solitary thoughts are clipped,
thorns have no fragrance.

Sometimes the words tumble,
mock their own arrangement
and mouth the vase.

It's a human-interest thing.
In the rush of the poem,
I pluck the burgeoning words,
arrange brittle petals in pots,
display my Jewish side.

The Hungry Conception

Words crept through
the bedroom window
on noisy spider legs,
danced under the ceiling
webs captured light
between silver and moon.

Heavy shadows draped over me
like woolen blankets.
Smothered dreams converged
into one huge appetite
for stars and chocolate.

Reaching for Mystery

(for Katherine L. Gordon)

In the virtual reality
of stirring life,
maiden dreams
swim the milky way
in an old bookstore.

A door opens in the stone
blocks out harsher geometry
in a contest of heroes
the spirit lions roar
become the wind and water
from an ancient forest.

In the spiral dance
of her ordered world
twilight and star-shadows
wait darkly beautiful
in the long ancestral night
under a fitful moon.

Roaming undefined space
her spirit, eagle-free
searches through the ashes for answers.

Testaments on desert mounds
blaspheme out of place
pierce the clear air
hold all secrets, songs of birds,
bread and wine and the seas.

Only the wolf
buries dried bones in a cloth of light,
no sleep can banish
this misty phantom.

In the drudge of the day
barefoot in a thorn-field,
she writes notes of longing
against all taboos,
holds the little volume
on the edge of her path
through a hemlock vision,
makes magic.

In Peggy's Garden

(In Memory of Peggy Fletcher)

Every flower-filled summer,
Peggy held poetry workshops
on wave-struck rock beds.
Life's ups and downs were patiently planted.
Cultivated rhythms dropped like flower seeds
with a dramatic thud.

Peggy followed the same routine
through coded paths of dot-coms.
She swooned over long-stemmed ideas
while strolling barefoot in her garden.

It was a universe of flesh,
crafted from rich soil
that penned the scent of lilacs.

Petals dropped one by one
while everyone feasted
under a canopy of green
in her small Eden.

Now, ragged grey skies
blanket Peggy's human garden
while her masterpieces blossom
under a heavy sun.

The Superstitious Moon

The most ancient astrological doctrine stated the moon governed the mouth. Peaks and valleys undiscovered smooth as butter, the inhabited space reminiscent of all that vents, resigned blue like yesterday's sky sighing wide.

The most ancient astrological doctrine stated the moon governed the brain. The core of the universe, past, present and future imprecise and distinctly different personalities and routines, a meteor in flight.

The most ancient astrological doctrine stated the moon governed the belly. Echoed the tides of a voice from a world I've never known, still linked, still bonding like a love song crooned again and again, retracing ocean views, gusts of wind, apertures in arguments the shaded place unscathed, without stars.

The most ancient astrological doctrine stated the moon governed the organs of reproduction. Rifts and lumps in the land of the photo men claimed their stake, smiling through plastic bubbles, square and sturdy astronauts embraced the moon, made love through telescopes, birthed new places in uncharted seas.

The most ancient astrological doctrine stated the moon governed the left eye of the male and the right eye of the female. Compulsiveness and subservience, difficult eye to eye contact, superficial mirror images rendering mysterious observations, intimidating language luminous and collapsing, the diversity in movement, the metaphorical dance invented by elliptical forces constantly revolving
because a moving object is harder to find.

The most ancient astrological doctrine stated the moon governed the female liver. For once, not inferior like gold on the meadow, deep, harmonic, in the digestive system. Like the solar system formed an orbit inside its own milky way. Molecules and foreign substances open like a starburst, leap from red to bright yellow, an army of light thrilling further and further into the dark. Bridges the rift between then and now in a continual flow.

The most ancient astrological doctrine stated the moon governed the left side of the body. Wrapped in mists beyond alien faraway worlds infinity divided the body in half, knocked on loose ashes, let in the rain and daffodils, surfaced onto light after a ten-hour spell the left side in the dark, misunderstood and ostracized, hanging on the tip anxiously governed by mankind.

Dreaming of Poetry

In the same dream
shouting stiff-lipped,
there is silence
grinding a dervish-night.

I pry open old poetry books
shuffled like cards in a deck,
on a table end-to-end.

I look for metaphor
inside every human exchange.

There is a list.
Don't ask me to describe it.

The universal intelligence
of mental brilliance shines
only when I am fast asleep.

Nocturnal Inspiration

Yellow spires of light
from one small candle flame
insert magnificence
on blank spaces.

The fallout lands in my lap.
I am writing
a brand new poem
in brilliant quietness

between fire and inspiration,
between nightfall and morning.

The Body as Landscape

A haze rises in a morning
surrounded by trees,
advances
like buffalo in a field,
fading before dawn.

A sift of light
evaporates in a wisp
like nothing ever happened.

One of those days
not so different from this
shadows went missing
in abandoned fields,
from finely spun skins.

Memory is stubbly grass, dry leaves,
a blank page
collected in clear plastic
the demise of sweet history
meager cadaver
rehashed, replayed.

In a moment or in an hour
the whole sky may blow,
breeze its way
through shudders of time,
swoop and dip in the landscape,
repeat the poem.

ABOUT THE AUTHOR

I.B. (Bunny) Iskov

Bunny is the Founder of The Ontario Poetry Society: theontariopoetrysociety.ca. Her work has been extensively published in literary journals and anthologies. In 2009, Bunny received the inaugural R.A.V.E. Award—Recognizing Arts Vaughan Excellence—for her work as Art Educator and Mentor in the Literary Arts. The award was presented in recognition of outstanding contribution to the cultural landscape of the City of Vaughan.

www.ingramcontent.com/pod-product-compliance
Ingram Content Group UK Ltd.
Pitfield, Milton Keynes, MK11 3LW, UK
UKHW020138250726
13967UKWH00002B/730